"We stopped looking for monsters under our bed when we realized that they were inside us."

-Charles Darwin

One of the greatest scientific discoveries of our
time is that there are two of you. Really! You
have two brains - a big one on top of a little one

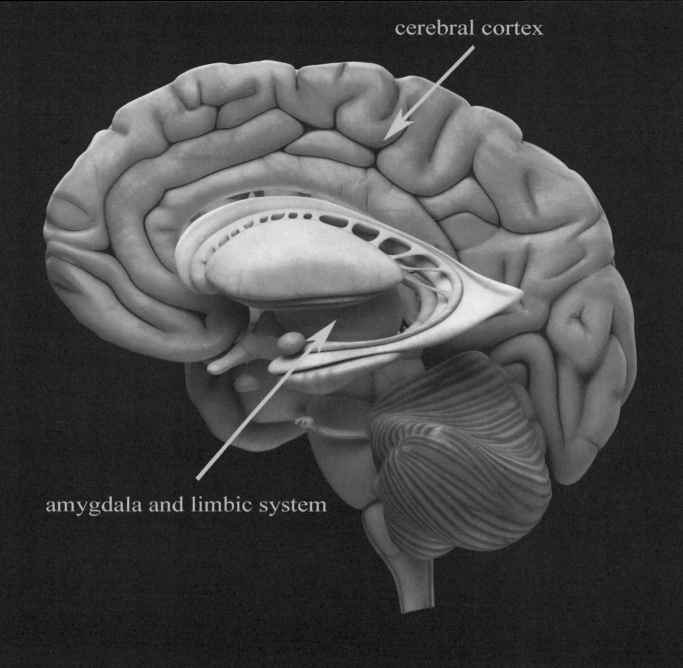

cerebral cortex

amygdala and limbic system

The big brain is the cerebral cortex and is the one reading this book. The little brain is the amygdala and the little parts around it. Each brain has its own thoughts, memories and personality.

All animals with back bones have the same
brain structure. These include mammals, birds,
reptiles, fish and amphibians. Humans have the
largest cortex (big brain) compared to body size.

Crocodilians are the smartest reptiles. My alligator, named Lucy, understands ten human words and is playful like a puppy.

The little brain is primitive and is where ou feelings come from. Reptiles also have an amygdala and emotions.

Why do we have two brains? Airplanes have
two pilots - the captain and copilot. The copilot is
there mainly for emergencies

The big brain is good at math and solving problems but it's too slow for dangerous situations. The amygdala is fast. It has something called the "fight or flight" response.

If a Komodo dragon races toward you it's your amygdala that tells you to either run away or poke it in the eyes when it bites your boot.

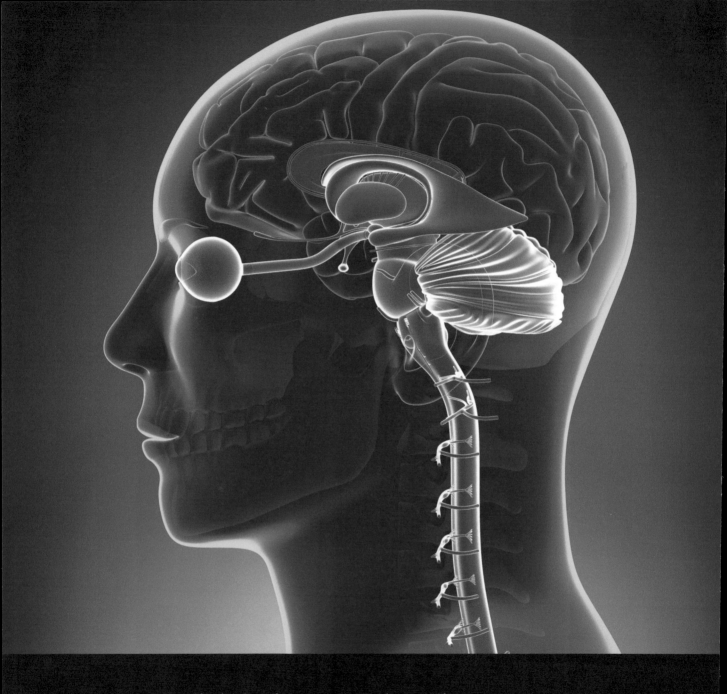

The little brain can see through your eyes. In one experiment researchers sat blind people in front of a computer screen. They showed pictures of human faces smiling or frowning. Amazingly, some of the blind people's expressions imitated the faces on the screen.

The little brain never forgets. Most people
dont't remember anything before the age of five,
but their amygdala does.

Fear is contagious. We get our fears when our amygdalas see others act afraid. Your big brain doesn't remember your parents acting afraid of snakes but the little brain does.

Anger also comes from the amygdala, the crocodile brain, and can be contagious. The purpose of anger is to help us fight back in dangerous situations and prevent abuse from others.

In most cases, anger is a bad thing that can hurt others and damage our bodies.

If the crocodile brain gets angry enough, it can knock out the pilot and hijack the plane. This is called a psychotic episode and it's when people do bad things. Sometimes people don't remember what they've done in this state. The Incredible Hulk is Hollywood's version of this.

But there's good news! Your big brain can
control the amygdala. My favorite TV show
growing up was Kung Fu. It was about a Kung Fu
master, named Caine, who came to the Old West
from China in the 1800's. People called him mean
names, picked fights with him and even spit in his
face and it didn't bother him.

Some buddhist monks can sit outside all night
long in freezing temperatures and not shiver.

It takes practice but next time you start getting angry just tell yourself it really doesn't matter and to stop being angry. It will take a minute to calm down but you can put the crocodile back in its cage.

Others can sense if you're good at controlling your crocodile. They will trust you more and you'll have more friends.

I think the amygdala is the biggest cause of
divorces and broken relationships. Every time you
allow yourself to become angry with a loved one
your amygdala remembers and this anger adds up
over time.

Eventually, it is impossible for the two of you
to be together. Just decide not to become angry
with loved ones. The amygdala never forgets

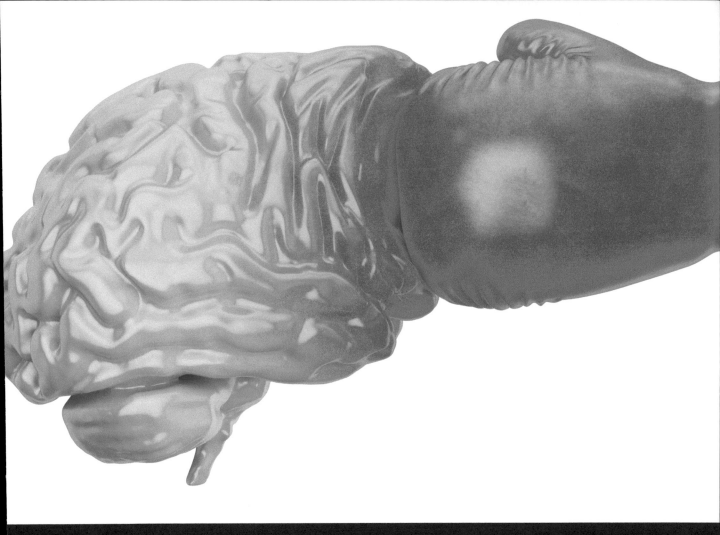

Brain damage can make it hard to control your anger. Your amygdala is controlled by the front part of your big brain - the frontal cortex.

The delicate brain cells connecting them can be easily damaged by a blow to the head.

The brain is like a bowl of jello inside a suitcase. If you shake it hard you might have a life time of emotional problems.

Wear helmets with sports and don't get into fist fights. Even hitting soccer balls with your head can hurt your brain.

Lead in your food and water can also damage your brain. Paint dust in older houses is the main cause of lead in children bodies.

Studies have shown that kids with lead in their bodies are more likely to end up in prison for violent crimes as adults. They couldn't control their emotions.

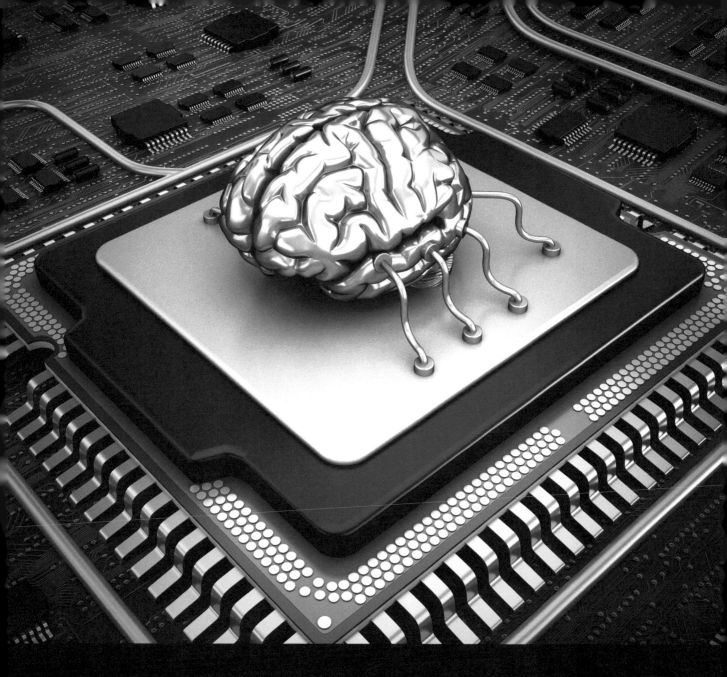

Culture is very important in controlling our little brain.

Culture is two things. It's rules and it tells you what's important. Culture is like the software you put on your computer. Your big brain is like the hard drive.

**CULTURE
RULES**

Every country or group of people has its own
culture. In America, boys don't wear dresses but
Scotland they do. We get our culture from our
parents, friends, television, movies and religion.

If a baby was raised in a cave by animals without culture they probably wouldn't be very fun to hang out with. This person would take something from you if they wanted it. They would hit you with a branch if you made them angry or didn't like them.

When we are born our big brain is like a blackboard with no writing on it. It has lots of space so culture can be written on it.

But the little brain is born with many instructions. The amygdala is programmed to seek a chemical called dopamine. It's candy for the crocodile.

Every time you eat sugar, play video games, or realize someone likes you - you get a squirt of dopamine and feel pleasure. The problem comes when the crocodile gets too much dopamine from one thing.

Addiction is when the copilot wants things like drugs or alcohol so much it becomes stronger than the pilot and hijacks the plane.

Alcohol ruins many lives and causes many cancers. If you start drinking alcohol there is a 22% (1 in 5) chance you will become an alcoholic.

I've never been drunk from alcohol or tried drugs. I just don't trust my crocodile.

Bad culture also makes it hard to control your little brain. Examples of bad culture are gangs and extremists. They say it's okay to hurt other people. When the big brain gets bad culture and teams up with the angry little brain then bad things can happen. This explains terrorists and drive-by shootings.

Bullying and racism come from our amygdala.
The little brain doesn't like people who are
different and is mean to them. In one experiment,
babies were less friendly to babies with different
skin color.

Good culture teaches us it's okay to be different. Animal species that are all the same (lacking genetic variation) are more likey to become extinct.

If someone bullies you just tell yourself it doesn't matter what they think and walk away. Don't let others control your emotions. You are not a puppet.

Ever wonder why some dreams are weird or hard to remember? Dreams come from the amygdala. The little brain has to stay awake at night to listen for danger. I think it gets bored and creates its own fantasies.

Sleep walking occurs when the amygdala takes control of the body while the cortex is turned off.

Why do we get scared watching horror movies?
The amygdala thinks the movie is real even though
your cortex knows it's not.

Action and horror movies are exciting for the
amygdala but there are probably better things to do
with your precious time.

Money doesn't buy happiness. When you go shopping and buy something your crocodile gets a shot of the pleasure chemical dopamine. But it wears off.

Many people spend their lives chasing dopamine and are not happy. Don't be a hamster on the dopamine wheel to nowhere.

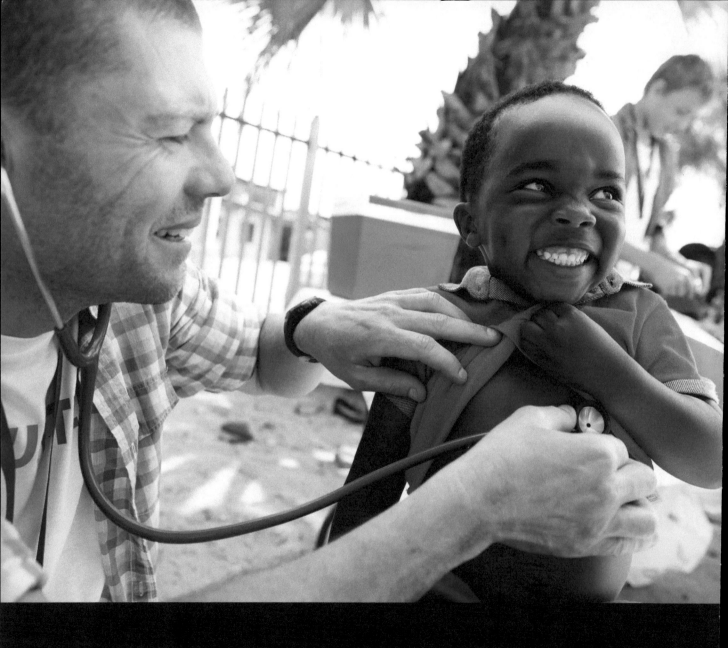

One good thing about our little brain is that it seems to be happiest when we help other people. This has been true in my life.

Be the boss of your crocodile and make the world a better place. That's the real secret to happiness.

SCOTT PETERSEN
THE REPTILE MAN

Scott Petersen has lectured to almost three
million people in the Pacific Northwest over the
last 30 years. He has appeared on nationally
televised shows Bill Nye The Science Guy and
PBS Biz Kids. He is the founder of The Reptile
Zoo in Monroe, WA. Scott is also a video
producer and his nature videos can be found at
www.reptileman.com.

CPSIA information can be obtained
at www.ICGtesting.com
Printed in the USA
BVHW022217200821
614852BV00003B/72